We Danced a Tango Red

Jeff Warren

 FriesenPress

Suite 300 - 990 Fort St
Victoria, BC, Canada, V8V 3K2
www.friesenpress.com

ISBN
978-1-4602-7308-1 (Hardcover)
978-1-4602-7309-8 (Paperback)
978-1-4602-7310-4 (eBook)

1. Poetry, Subjects & Themes, Love & Erotica

Distributed to the trade by The Ingram Book Company

TABLE OF CONTENTS

I
Secrets of the Breeze

III
I Sing On Your Cake

IV

Are You Going to Embrace That Hamburger?

V
Street Beast

DEDICATION

To those whom I have loved and who loved me
back, however long—however brief.

ACKNOWLEDGMENTS

I wish to express my love and gratitude to Maeve McConnell who has inspired so many of my words, and who has edited all of them.

I
Secrets of the Breeze

Secrets of the Breeze

I've found a dress for you to wear
A Renaissance raiment
in a secret catalogue
I once acquired
You'll don it for the beach
and underneath you'll be

naked

You see, I want you to feel
the salty breeze as it laps across

your thighs

And I will be next to you
looking into your eyes

Through the Blinds

Through the blinds
come zebra stripes

dancing shadows
across your sunlit body
lying languidly
across my bed

beckoning me

to eclipse
the golden ones between

High Tide

In the mouth of my cave
we stood in silence
but for the rhyme of roiling waves
washing clean the rocks at shore
and your tender look
bathed my longing soul
Your face shone silken silver blue
under the soft light
of our full-faced moon
and I could hear my heart
above the ocean's seething swirl
Sweet Heaven help me...
a day later
I am blinded and deaf
to all reason...
all sense and wonder...
to all...
but the miracle
of the moonlight
that shone in your eyes

White on White

you were all in white

languishing

a white crucifix floating
on the whitecloud carpet

the moment erased all colors
blinding me from time
blinding me from all
but the glory of your face
hands
and your naked feet

Nocturne

In dreams have I come to you
to walk this earth and chart the stars
to laugh and write my songs
to find a sunset
for us to kiss in
and to sleep in your arms

Trainscontinentalism

Forty years
have I loved you
forty years
and now I feel you
coming to me
across the miles

Across time

Along steel rails and the heartbeat
of the thundering pulsing beat
of the wheels beneath you
as you wonder and elate
at this new life of yours...
and mine

Come kiss me
die with me
but first...
live with me for forty years more

Inamorata

My lover is secret

My lover's secret
is me

We kiss is in still shadows
in unlit streets

We hide
in deep dark dreams

Remembrance

I remember with haunting stillness
Your slight and limber frame

The miracle white
Of your perfect belly

The tantalizing beauty
Of your grace
As you lay silent
Faint of breath

Innocent and serene
In love with life

We Danced a Tango Red

We danced a tango red
as hot as running blood

Now blow me a kiss
across the universe
and hum a waltz with me

Polaris

through fathoms of fear
and a course unmapped
you are magnetic north…

the needle of my compass
unwavering
across bootblack seas
points to you

Gaze Bayward

Take it in, take in the still beauty of it
let it fill you…momentarily
Let me snatch you back
out from that reality
into another for just a moment
stolen from that perfect view

One moment

which is mine
and none other's

a moment when—
for even just a flash
you are touched
by what you see
 in my eyes

and your breath halts

after that
you can spend the day
bay-gazing

Hues

I am dark
I know this

and you are light
I say

so mix with me
in rapture

and let us play
as gray

Goddess of the Olfactory

Where comes
this haunting and illusive scent
of impending passion?
You wear it as a signature
of your patrician mystery
Calling to me
Drawing me
Luring me
Ever closer

And we have not yet finished our salads

Caron Poivre begins to fade
As night beckons us to—
withdraw
to less public eyes
Subtle floods bring springs
of new sensation
Sensations lingering
and wafting in partnership
With those of your own invention

Animal-pungent richness

Ethereal intoxication…

Morning dew and Starbuck's robust roast
usher a new day
bathing us in salmon pink

And I am blinded
by The Goddess of Light
and scents recalled

Love Quilt

I long for the moment when as you rise
naked
from our tousled bed I can see

the embossed pattern of concentric
wedding rings

carved in the soft curve of your alabaster back

Exaltation

my swallow sings
in your sacred bush
with flicking wings
for you to flush

we taste the sweet
elixir's night
as spirit greets
our flesh's flight

and so to fly
we both consume
with breathy sigh
to prick the moon

but suns will rise
to light the way
my poem's guise
and   me   at   play

Tigress

Dare not
under God's fierce frown
to tread upon
nature's innocent bloom
for the wrath of fire
and scourge endure
should harm befall
the sweet issue
of my blood

Argentine Tango

'Tis the devil's dance
a dance of danger
Little One
for those who have tasted
the sting of wickedness
on their lips

It will seduce you
without ruth
and turn your eyes
to hot pursuits
writhing its searing tendrils
through your soul
until you become
it's branded bride

Beware…

Sweet Creature

on this the eve
of your womanhood
of what and whom
you give your passion
unless you are prepared
to see the sin
within your portrait

Stillframes

I remember you by inches
and see you now in

stillframes

recalling your grace
your hair in the wind
the deep dark eyes
that looked into me
the lips that took my breath away

Two trees

We are as two trees
In an enchanted grove
Planted far apart
Nourished
By the twinkle of stars

Roots deeply embedded like thirsty tongues
Writhing to the waiting tendrils of the other
Drunk on the moist and fragrant elixir
of peat and earth
Tasting the sweet essence
Of soil and soul

Night brings growth
And naked moon-soaked limbs reach
To engulf…
Entwine…
And tangle
In fierce communion…

Laced against Heaven's Sky

Signatures

Melt, meld
Lithe and liquid...
Legato

Press to me
Be one with me...
Appassionato

Soar to strains
As yet unheard…
Accelerando

Lost breath
Hearts aquiver…
Diminuendo

Whisper now
And into sleep...
Pianissimo

Benediction

Meet me in some small beach town
along the coast
and I'll build a shrine
around your footprint
in the sand

All Words Be Thine

All that I pen
is yours

any words to them
were yours first

for you see if I loved else
it were but for thee
and the you
I found
in
other's smiles

II
Ash and Smoke

Ash and Smoke

If you will not turn me
into ash and smoke
then find some
secret place
to hide me
from the dark

The light of your eyes?

Cyberlove and Other Fantasies

Heed this warning, all who seek
the mirrored reflection of their secret souls
through this electronic window
this vast...

unplace.

Be warned that you will succeed only briefly
to build and believe the E-dream.
You can learn more in six hours
than you can in six months, it is true.
Instant connection and fulfillment...
Instant exchange of love and desire.

But the autobiography

one sends

and receives

is entirely self-selective.

Nothing of scars,
scabs
and Devil Worship.

Good for a limited time only

Brand

I will memorize what you said of me
and caption my soul with it…

each and every word

a tattoo perhaps…of Celtic implication
a brand…burned deep into my flesh.

I accept your words of love and hate
dismay...
and truth

Kelp

why are you winking at me from behind that undulating
bed of kelp
why will you not let me swim ahead and out of your reach
why must I hold your tender seductive glance
why could you not have lived in the world
your auburn tresses catching the sunlight instead of
tangling
around me
snaring me
soothing me
sucking me
to your naked breast
your siren smile
your unearthly chant

Soon

a mystic word
indefinite and cruel
a word of maybe
might be
wait

fuck soon
fuck agony
fuck longing
fuck soon
a word ethereal
distant and vague

fuck now

now
real
honest and touchable
white breasts
naked
heaving

now

Jilt Kit

seduce
ensnare
and otherwise corrupt

then

when you catch it picking its nose
call its character into question

then

leave
the little snot
naked abed

then

with an odor of sanctity
march to the door
and slam it behind you

Pieta

what is this thread
that connects your soul to mine?

the sadness in your eyes
runs in my veins like a
black river

and there is nothing
I am allowed to do

there is no whimpering
in your regal face
only a somberness
devoid of pity

I kneel at your feet
wanting beyond explanation
to pay tribute to your image
and to let you know what I see

to cradle your hurt
to bring light to your face
would be the ultimate fusion

for in drinking your tears
I nourish my own reason for being

Hangover

I drank beyond my capacity
and now I don't
remember
who
we
were

Winter in Northfield

Are you preparing for a cold Minnesota winter?
Is there wood for the fire and extra quilts for the bed?

The snows are a comin', Love
with a vengeance
The winter chill is nigh upon us

Find a warm heart I beg
and thoughts too
'til the thaw

New Year's Eve

I woke this morning to comfort you
from the awful fight we had in the night
you without sleep
you without your medication
and I still trembling
from the hurts we made

before my glued eyes could open
I felt my hand upon something
warm and satin smooth
warm and smooth
as the body that had just
molted
the red silk pajamas that I had given you
a mere week ago

in candlelight

the puddle next to me
was violent scarlet
spilt
against the bleached white sheet
like a slowly spreading bloodstain

...the last relic of our severed love

Eulogy

are we then to remain silent
trusting and living on memory alone?

I rejoice

in the wealth
of you
here in my mind's eye...

alive in my soul's
casket

Dark Dreams

I woke from dreams this morning
and I knew...
God, help me, I knew...
I loved you less

A cold crystalline pane
separates us
until I can barely see your face
or hear your voice

I fought so hard
with my own fierce love
and my own dream
I tried to sing my way to you
through the lie

I am sinking into oblivion
the thing I feared most
I reach out for your hand
something to bring me back
from the numb stillness
the fading into night

I don't want you to be
a fading memory
I was a man reborn in you
and yet my songs and my dreams
go unechoed

and I sense the impending
atrophy of my soul

I am sinking
I am drowning
I am dying
read what we were
read our dreams
and you will understand
that I could not accept less
than what we found
in each other's words
in one another's arms

I may now die alone
I am not afraid of dying
only afraid of having never lived

I have lived in you.

Angel of Mercy
let me sleep
do not let me awaken
to loving her less
rather
let me never waken
from
my
dreams

My Muse

What a versatile muse are you
inspiring me in hatred
as well as
the other thing

Kimono Red

hanging listless alone

waiting

dead in the night black

waiting

dawn light through louvered slats
streaks across fine crimson silk
and jewel threads of silver and gold
white embroidered herons
sail skyward like paper kites
shadows sharpen in anticipation

waiting
for my lover
there to be wrapped
within

Fleurs Bleu

I sat staring at the flowers you gave
in hues of varied blue
and wondered at the universe
and how that color dominates

The sky of course
and certainly the sea

The palette of your eyes

My heart
when you don't see me

Divorce

It's one thing to be alone...

Totally Solo

and it is quite another matter to be legally alone
so tell me again...
what is the difference
between being legally blind and just plain blind? and is
plain insane anything akin to being certified, I wonder?

It's over now

I got what I wanted

I am but one
a severed couple
half of us is gone

The Unrequited

now I know that what you felt
was not passion
at least passion for me
at least for the real me

I kept us afloat and buoyed
by the effusion and blind obsession
that burned in me
but did not burn in you

this was no shortcoming of yours alone
we both wanted it too much
we did what we had to do
to perpetuate...
to believe the dream

it was not reality that did us in
it was not the practical issues of

time

distance

or even children and dogs

it was fear

of
the
dream
coming true

The Promise

an empty thing

      vacant as dry air

stillborn

    worth not the real and tangible hope
held to my sore heart

Satin Sheets

There is chill in the air
I pulled the satin sheets
from off our bed today
and washed them
in a cycle
delicate-cold
...
I hung them from a branch
of our favorite tree
there to dance in
the autumn breeze
until the wind
had kissed them dry
...
In sad remembrance
I placed our virgin sheets
in the oaken chest
with the silken raiments
you never wore
...
Soft russet flannel
now dresses our altar
awaiting tender love
that will never come again

And the winter snows draw nigh upon us

Let's Do Brunch

We met for brunch

greasy buffet fare

I wanted to tell you I cared
but you had your own agenda

So we sat

and said nothing
over wilted eggs and rancid ham

Queen of Hearts

For Princess Diana

I knew you
your clear and tender eyes
your lithe figure
out of place
in the sights of greedy gawking peers
who tried to live through you
an icon of hope and courage
they could never touch

You were hunted and ravaged
assailed by blinding explosions
of light
tabloid freeze-frames
feasting
on your delicate soul
sucking on your virtue
newsprint
flat and grey and hueless
blanking the mystery blue
of your perfect eyes

The commonwealth
will weep and wail
and mourn their loss
grieving the symbol
they made bastard
blaming you for

leaving them
in poverty
alone
with the horror
of their own emptiness
I know you

Royal Grace

Would that I might lay down
a carpet of unknown color
at your feet
to soften and guide your journey
into the glory of
golden light
and the anthem of angels

Blank Canvas

After all is said and done, I can tell you this:
It was not your soul I loved, but the one I painted upon you
My own portrait of what I wanted to see

The paint is faded, cracked and peeled
but the images rendered
if not true
are indelibly real
on the canvas
of my memory

Crucifixation

For Christmas
you gave me a Celtic cross
even as you knew
I was a devout Atheist.
Did you think my love of giving and my love of ancient
pagans
would lure me into leaving the gruesome symbol
of your malevolent god on the night stand?

Diminishing Returns

so in love we were
pure and final it was
the ultimate conclusion
of souls in search of light

then the night came

The Intensity of Silence

I heard "*Silence is Golden*"
your silence is not golden

your silence is a mad cacophony of ...

nothing
limbo
demons dark

sound shadows eclipsing me in eternal deafness and dread still

The Last Word

In the name of charity
and what might have been…
I beg of you
read this volume but once
in solitude

Gather up all relics which bound us
all sounds
images
smells
memories
and in ceremony grave
with ruthless and glorious blaze
pay one last tribute
to what we were

Send my soul as coiling smoke
into the black beyond
and

oblivion

III
I Sing On Your Cake

I Sing On Your Cake

Rich and buttery
Smooth and sweet
Melting down
From so much heat

Oozing loose
From off your cake
Rich confection
Mine to take

When You Kiss a Frog

When you kiss a frog
upon the lips
and send your magic
through his soul
we all know what happens
by legends told

But if the frog is old
with sagging skin
and foggy eyes,
what then?

If his ribbit is coarse
when he croaks
and he hops arthritically
when you love him for what he is
and the love you have transforms him
will the prince be young or old?

Perhaps we'll never know

Kaleidoscope

I've found a spectrum
never seen before

an array of light
that transcends color

sweeping splashes of harmony of our two selves

transportation of a new kind
dazzling and poignant shades
lost and weightless in simple truth

and my eyes are closed

Unstandard Time

What idiot thought this up?

Different time zones-- there is nothing standard about it
Eastern-central-mountain-pacific-my-ass

I will not answer to some higher-being prankster who thinks
He or She can limit the expression of my soul to a goddam
Fucking Stopwatch

I am no fool. I will find the place where my past
and your future can embrace

And no one will watch us

Jessica McClintock

You lure me in tantalizing and helpless seduction
Intoxicating fumes taunt
And I swoon into blissful reverie

Should I go blind
I could find you
across the universe

Ode to a Naked Tummy

In you walk
your midriff naked
No Venus ever offered
a more perfect apparition

The shirt tails
tied in a sailor's knot
drape limp above
your jewel-like navel
and classic curves

My breathing halts
as I watch your belly rise
undulate and purr
with sensual rhythm

Jeans cut just low
so as to taunt me
into a waking dream
of unbearable longing
and curiosity

Marionette

My lonely little prancing doll
lift your head with pride
and smile into the sun
and trace the air
with graceful arms
sing my song just once
arrogant and free
and dance for me

Heart Specialist

I approach the white Formica counter
early
to be examined
to be seen
she is looking down deep into her keyboard
her painted fingers so adept that I can feel them tickling me

waiting to be seen...

I wait...

she looks up

a shock-wave of warm air fills my lungs and I cannot exhale

her eyes widen
she smiles

and I wonder why I am floating as in a dream
and I wonder why I cannot remember my name

or why I am here

or if I just died

not that it matters

Half Full

I am drunk on your words.
for you touched me as tenderly
as if you had kissed my eyelids
and took communion in my tears.

I think I can face anything now
Yes, even the thought of
your beautiful face
evaporating
into
the
gossamer mist

Gone Fishing

I found a lustrous pearl
that in an oyster lied
it promised pretty treasures
if I would peek inside

I found a pure pink pearl
in an oyster open wide
it promised poignant pleasures
if I would come inside

In warm and soothing waters
as deep as dark blue night
I found my lover dancing
with aching love delight

I found the perfect haven
in soft and haunting sighs
the art of being god
while un-guised in your eyes

Lone Ranger

I am
   in a circle
     looking out
       beyond
         my own
           circumference
             into the borders
            of myriad
       other circles
     which are
   not me.
I am the center
  of my circle,
    the pivot point
       equidistant from
          a continuous
        curving edge
      not exceeding
    my walls.
My universe
  is complete.

Garbo & Gilbert

It was a day like today
there was weather
the chill was invigorating
and the damp was cleansing
and we were warm
arm in arm
you...were Garbo
and I was Gilbert

and the passersby knew it
because we exuded it

and for a moment suspended
dear soul
we were what we wanted to be

and now plucked from time
for consumption when we most need it

we have it again

how I adored you

...now remember to breathe

Fences

Come, my boy
and let me lift you
over the high fence
I have been on the other side
and I know a shortcut
to wonder

The Wizard

He can dazzle with magic
as he struts onto a stage
of rough-hewn planks
washed in amber light

He can draw the breath of onlookers
by simple
                          sleight-of-hand

He can astonish by his forceful vision
He can frighten with tenderness
He can conjure sorrowful tears
                          and tears of joy
He can turn a mundane collection of cloth
into mantles of sublime nobility

He can spin yarns of wondrous castles dragons and fools

but he cannot temper the ultimate reality
                          of time...

and he cannot
make you
love
him

Fantasies

if fishers had not dreamt up mermaids
those sirens of the sea
we land boys would have done
believe you me

Eye of the Beholder

a kite let loose
the sound of children at play
the crack of a bat on an autumn night
the giant mountains of the west
a salmon-amber sunset
the look that Garbo gave to Gilbert
Rachmaninoff and Art Nouveau
a Celtic brooch
any strand of your auburn hair
the underarch of your shoeless foot
those dimples in your back
your naked tapered legs...
all mine

The Tree House

High and scary
was my secret aerie
nestled in the gnarly branches
of the giant
Chinese elm

A haven
A hideout
A haunt
where my thoughts and dreams
could incubate

in private

Dreams of flying skyward

Dreams of high school girls
in tight skirts

Visions of daring deeds
and being grown-complete

Go back there with me
We will wrap the world around us
and make a place where completeness
is in each other's arms

Every Man's Mermaid

no lower limbs to lie in
no real air to breathe
only the mystic
need
to swim amniotic
and nest
in dreams

The Old Actor

The vintage model is he
Strong of spirit even if supported on arthritic knees
Mystery still gleams in his eye
There is magic in the graceful curves
that his wrinkled hands trace upon the air

The warm and resonant baritone that once sang true
bears a husky hoarseness now
but yet can shake the timbers as it echoes in the hall
juddering the rafters

and soaring into the night sky

See him in his heyday
Remember him in light

The Norske Love

In quietude she sits
In the stock-still sea
Boot black sails
Rapt in solitude
Etched against
The haunting
Lunar face
Waiting…

For what may come

The FireStarter

asleep the earth
cool and dormant still
…waiting

birth of the mind
a point of sensation
a spark so tiny as yet not seen
a flash then signals through the night
and dark awakens

man is born as god
and there is light
pulsing embers
embryos
about to live
about to burst

earth's gift
searing momentum
writhing hot
so we can see
and bathe in warmth

or perish in blindness

Devil Moon

A white bisque moon winked at us
as we knit together
naked
under our clothes

pine and salt alive in the cool night air
whiskey on your breath
and mischief in your eyes

The Comma

The comma
is a form of punctuation
which has constantly baffled
me. One never knows when or
how to use the damned things
and besides they look like
stupid little tadpoles
with silly
little
tails

,

Psssst

hey…pssst… c'mere
I wanna show you something…

something magical

it's all right, really…and wonderful strange!

come…
come closer…
shhhh…it's a secret
but I will show just you…
pssst…look!
Butterfly wings
in colors n'er seen!

Dreamcatcher

Am I to be damned for loving
beyond my capacity
the youthful spirit of my seasoned soul...

Spring to my fall
Summer to my Winter nights...

will you kiss me gently
when we meet in my dreams?

The Poem Factory

Sit.   Close eyes.

      Breathe deep.

Conjure.

Bring forth her distant face into the mind's eye
And begin typing

IV
Are You Going to Embrace That Hamburger?

Are You Going To Embrace That Hamburger?

You're looking at that thing
as though it will bring you to climax.
The hungry lust in your eyes—
that voracious greed
you once held for me
now directed
to a double
greasy
piece
of
meat

Old Man's Music

(I hear a symphony)

Scratch his Bach
Ravel in his Scriabin
and he'll make a Faure
into your Debussy
Rock man in off
Peter Ilyitch

Non Sonnet

Shall I compare thee to a Shakespeare sonnet
of languid rhyme with syrup on it?

Will my words engender love
supplying hope from far above?

Or might they fall too coarse and flat
benumbed and trite
           missing you
           and where you're at?

Father Time

If I am so damned OLD
Don't you think your youthful self
ought to hurry up
and taste this vintage port
before it taints in a dank cellar?
The longer you wait
Sweet Wonder...
the shorter the time left us.

In the larger scheme of things
I hasten to add--
Considering the millennia
that have tick-tocked before us
what is a decade or two
amongst friends?

Play with me
Laugh with me
while you may

Naughty

Nibble, nipple squeeze and fondle
lick my wick and light my condle

Squat and crouch and lie down flat
Let me kneel where you just sat

Words taboo and not sublime
But finally Dear, I've made a rhyme

Sushi Queen

Man, can you put it away!
Where is Guinness when you need him?
I should have thought a first date would reveal
a daintier appetite.
God, is this a portent of things to come?
Duck sauce in your cleavage--
ginger in your hair--
me at the ATM
looking for ways
to finance the operation.
You looked a good deal slimmer on the Internet

The Middle-School Mafia

The paid security guards
                         duck for cover
as the mini-syndicate struts by in unison
decked in studied bouncer black and blue
with smirking kissers and cockscomb coifs
scanning their effect through anonymous shades

A chorus of Disneyesque ditties
                         sounds doings dire
The little clique of steel-toed teddy bears
checks each pooping pager
and quickly huddles in covert conference

When the coast is clear
the Big 8th Gang
yawns and swaggers into class
                         to bivouac in the back row
With zippered lips
they slide-ooze-slouch into their desks
asserting Territorial Imperative...
then to ponder the meaning of life...
and to calculate the minutes
before the big meeting

 at Baskins Robbins

The Cleaning Lady

My cleaning lady
is a clinging lady
and so...
I had to let her go

My Kitten

My kitten loves to be called "my kitten"
My kitten purrs and coos when she hears her name
My beautiful kitten arches in a graceful curve
when with my nails I scratch her back
My kitten is my very special pussy
My kitten purrs like a bathtub motorboat
when I pet her belly

My kitten is my sweetest love

My kitten is five feet eight
drives a red pickup
and works for the government

Your Dog Is Humping My Tuxedo

Now you know why
I never take you
to the opera

Mortise & Tenon

death to androgyny!
death to equality and sameness
down with similarity
and to hell with the alike

I protrude where you do not
and you in turn are hollow
I love your dovetail
my joint is yours to swallow
a dado for your daddio

Wet Poem

slick and damp
and juicy streams
melting fuse
of nectar creams

lapping tongues
and hunger slake
thirsty souls
of heaven take

wet and wild
with loins afire
drown with me
in damp desire

after we do sip the flower
I think we both
will need a shower

The Apostate

At six I was a skeptic
At nine I was an agnostic
At sixteen I was bad-mouthing the lord
At twenty-two I was the anti-christ
At thirty-five none of it mattered
But if you believe in the big guy...

Then perhaps I should look into it

Blisslessness

I will never use the word
"bliss"
in a poem

Four Little Munchkins

Four little Munchkins
All in a row
Two by two
Down the lane they go

One quite tall
While three are small
Whistling tunes
The clouds do call

Four little munchables
Sweet and cute
Gamboling free
To the piper's flute

Ice cream badges
Each do wear
Red flushed faces
And wind-blown hair

Forty bittyniblets
Pedaling bikes
Big breathy huffs
From joyful tykes

Golden streams
From end of day
Four little Munchkins
 Off to play

To Guys Who Have Not Been With A Fat Lady

Listen up gentleman
this is important
(even if not the time nor place)
For all of you who are chubbyphobic
get over it
you have NO IDEA

Mr. Rubens had something there
Mr. Rubens had undoubtedly
explored the depths
of feminine gelatin
the feast of folds and furrows
the pillowy-jiggley-jellowy-billowy-bulbous
thrills therein
Look again at a painting or two
you're in for a treat

Before you die
find a rotunda
and discover what I affectionately refer to as
the trampoline effect
Mister, trust me
the rewards are immense

God & Associates,
Anatomical Architects

The mind is nearest Heaven

                    and the feet are closest to the Earth

and along the centerline
exactly midway between them
we find the organs that connect the two.

Fucking brilliant!

Oldies But Goodies

Let's play "Mommies and Daddies"
I'll be Daddy

What say we kill each other off
by spending about a week and a half
doing the horizontal dance of the ages
Hell, a fortnight even
if we take our pills

Let's meet the big guy in the sky
locked together like Siamese twins
with great big grins
and our boots off

That Lady Has your Legs!

I saw your legs today
in the Santa Barbara Station

Nice young lady purchasing a ticket to…
Hollywood?

Framed against the aging walnut wainscoting
as she stood at the window awaiting change
Magnificent they were
Exactly replicated
from thigh to sandaled toes

Cool and corporal texture
Lithe and loving-limber
Half-browned
Firm and smooth
God's perfect architecture
My once and awesome sanctuary

I longed to caress them
(to apply the true test of authenticity, mind you)
But the S.B. Police
and the lady herself
would not have understood

Distant Darling
Tell me true
Were you in Santa Barbara today
…under an assumed face?

Waterbed

all hands on deck
lower the mains'l
swash yer buckles
hoist the miz'nmast
and let's be naughtycal

Just Friends

Return to our program of friendship
You said…wisely
We are going much too fast
and
We mustn't lose our perspective…you purred
And above all
No more poems!

I concur entirely

This non-poem is merely to state and confirm
our good and rational arrangement
I will curtail
I shall desist
Resist
And otherwise vacate the expression of
My abject
And raw desire
To be deep…
Ever so deep…

O…never mind

Scotch Induced Stupor

find me
i am so easy to find
i am found in you last breath

                            i am therein the backgr\ound
watching you asd you feed the chidren
and alone at night in that little circle of light
wher eyou go to sew
and I knowhen you are blue
and I sense when you are tinking aboit me
an wondering wat wenr wrong/

       look close
to your hart
find me
  god damn it

nthing is irreversabel

Poet-in-law

     e e cummings

          went

             so

               far

                 right

        that

nothing

        was

left

Why Do Doggies Love Me?

Why do doggies love me
when I just loathe them so?
Pooch's smooches make me sick
and yet they love to flicker-lick
their hungry tongues so dank and rank
across my thankless ugly mug.

Why do canines smell like that?
Have they been gnawing day-old rat…
or even worse, dead tabby cat?
What makes them stink to heaven high
enough, I think, to make one cry?
And of all the ills god might arrange
have you ever seen one as deranged
that grew as gruesome as the mange?

They come in all distorted sizes,
hairy-scary and cutsie guises…
from lean and mean with drooling lips
to ribboned queens with coiffured hips.

I nearly holler when I spy a collar
that cost more dollars
than my watch from Swatch
but I say nothing to the dog
for fear he'll dine upon my crotch!

In spite of hatred that goes bone deep
they come in packs and herds like panting birds

to wallow and swallow with deep moans hollow
to pay tribute at my feet

"Off you curs, you mongrels stinky," I bark at them...
and they just arf and yip and yap and lick my lap (eeyouuuuu)!
It's my mishap that dogs are kinky but why they love me
I will never know especially when I hate them so.

Politically Correct

I
sincerely
hope
this poem
didn't offend
anyone

V
Street Beast

Street Beast

The city is antiseptic and modern
mirrored structures angle
into the pewter sky
in exaggerated perspective.
legions of beings in columnar trails
march briskly along concrete paths
darting into cantilevered towers
to take their places behind anonymous windows.

Shrouded in army surplus
the street bum lugs his bundles along the boulevard.
toward his territorial bus bench.
His tattered woolen overcoat
the color of damp earth
hangs below the open knees
of his baggy trousers.

A crowd of nostrils flares
as the man's presence permeates the street corner.
The traffic signal changes colors
and the cologned colony escapes
into air-controlled sterile structures.
The man huddles into the bus bench
with his goods pulled close to his side
their bulk obliterating
a brightly lettered advertisement.

He absently gropes through several layers of clothing for his
bottle.
He studies its contents without enthusiasm
then takes a measured gulp
and returns the bottle to an interior pocket.
His bearded leathery face shows nothing.
His dark dead eyes stare down into the gutter.
The sun sets on the great city

bringing incandescent night.
The man unmoved
arms himself against the coming chill
with a long swig of cheap wine.
He pulls his coat's collar tight
over his wrinkled throat

When the sky turns its blackest
the street bum arranges his bundles under the bench
shaping a rough mattress.
He crawls into the lair
then wrapped warmly
in discarded financial journals
he sleeps.

The city gleams.
Quartz-light blankets the pavements with artificial sun
The tinny rattle of a gimpy grocery cart
punctures the quiet night.
The stroboscopic flash of headlamps
counterpoints the rickety rhythm
of the cart's three working wheels

as it limps along the avenue.
Shuffling behind the cart
are two rag wrapped feet.
The wheels retard
as they approach the bus bench.

The dormant mass under the seat shifts slightly
and the newsprint crackles like crunching leaves
The cart wheels halt
the bound feet frozen in mid-motion
The tense silence is broken
by a low rumbling snore.
as the cart inches bravely closer.
A filthy gnarled hand
sheathed in a fingerless glove

places a florist's rose upon the bench.
The bony fingers softly trace
the petals with reverence.
Then the metallic sound of the cart
jangles away and into the night.

As the first chromium tower is ignited by sun's dawn
the street bum stirs in his lair
He unscrews the cap from his bottle
and takes a ritual slug
He bundles the paper bedding and rises slowly
Looking down, he spies something
on the seat of his bench.
The flower trembles slightly in the early morning breeze.
The bum emits a grunt
and with the sweep of a giant paw
brushes the rose into the gutter.
He sits staring vacantly at the accelerating stream of traffic.

The crazy lady roots through the public waste
separating breakfast from yesterday's debris.
That she' is thirty-five or eighty-five is equally believable.

The true color of her hair is indiscernible.
Her powdered face and rouged cheeks
frame a pair of oddly hopeful eyes.
Her awkwardly painted lips
curl into a surreal smile.
She wears two dresses.
A drab shirtwaist serves as an uneven petticoat
to the gaudier dress she wears on the outside.
Over both she wears a man's open front sweater
with one button in the wrong buttonhole.
One arm bears a dried-up wrist corsage.

She stuffs some trash into the grocery cart
adjusts a brassiere strap
and continues her morning rounds.

One corner of the city is taken up by a florist.
In front of the entrance
baskets teeming with flowers
crowd the pavement
in hopes of tempting passersby.
The bag lady brings the cart to a stop
amongst the colorful bouquets.
She fills her lungs with the thick,
sweet aroma.
With unquestioning audacity
she filches a perfect long-stemmed rose.
From the edge of the basket
she snaps up a piece of the green tissue
that is always included
at no extra charge.
She wrings it around the stem of the rose
then turns to place it in the cart.
An unwelcome pigeon is perched on the push-bar
grooming itself.
The mad woman swats at the intruder
sending it aloft
in a flailing frenzy.
She spits out vicious curses
then pushes the cart down the street
muttering self-righteously.

The street bum senses an alien presence
as the crazy lady nears him.
He ejects a territorial growl
but she is lost on her own strange stage.
whispering
to some illusive audience.

Suddenly
without connection
she turns back to the man on the bench.
He catches the last moment of her glance

before she is led away
by some ethereal mystery.

Deep in the darkness of an unlit street
the bum paws through a wire rubbish basket.
Finding nothing of use
he shuffles on
stopping only to quench his thirst.
He walks the city aimlessly for hours
until he is met with the specter
of his own image in a rectangle
of plate glass.
He does not recognize the primitive man before him.
He steps cautiously toward the image.
A flash of dazzling light
momentarily blinds him.

Before him is a fine jewelry store.
The display window is trimmed with simple elegance.
Behind the two-inch plate glass
grows a single silk rose in a slim crystal vase.
Nested within its petals
is the spark of light
a brilliant diamond.
He reaches toward it.
His greasy hand is stopped by the cold glass.
He leans in toward the pane
where he comes face to face
with a hollow lifeless stare...

The street bum sits as usual on the bus bench.
The tinkling music of the cart
seems almost playful
on this day as it nears the bench.
Its lunatic pilot
sporting a tulle turban in madder violet
mumbles something about the color of the sky.

She stops behind the bench.
In a little girl's voice
she chants a mad litany.
The man on the bench takes a long draw on his bottle.
Caught up in her insane reverie
the woman begins to dance
to music only she can hear.
The street bum belches.
A pair of mating flies lights on his matted beard.
The crazy lady digs from her rubble
a fractured hand mirror.
The haunted dance continues
as the woman gazes at the cracked reflection of Aphrodite.
The little girl's voice becomes breathy and faint
and finally is consumed
by the sound of a flatulent bus.

She sighs.
Her contented face is flushed and alive.
She laps the sweat from the back of her hands.
Crouching
to the bottom shelf of her old cart,
she picks out the long-stemmed rose.
Rising
she draws in a long breath of its intoxicating smell.
She drops the rose
on the bench
next to the street bum,
then with a tittering giggle
she hurries away.
The bum expels a low rumbling grunt.
He looks at the flower,
then with a swift move sweeps it off the bench
onto the sidewalk.

An onslaught of cordovan wing-tips
and chic feminine pumps

crushes the flower deep into the pavement
until it resembles a pressed keepsake.
After a time
the man unaccountably rises from the bench
staring at the squashed flower.
The commuters file by on either side of him
as he kneels next to it.
He carefully picks up the rose
which leaves a stained silhouette in the concrete.
The bum returns to his bench,
cradling the broken rose
in his crusted hands.

It is late night.
in the tiled plaza.

At the base of twin towers
gushes a great fountain.
From its center
rises an abstract twisted sculpture.
Neon light shimmers
on the planes of rusting steel.
Chlorinated water
trickles from its angular mass.

The bum
weighted with his bundles
walks heavily toward the fountain.
For a long time he sits motionless
on the edge of the pool.
Then he moults the many layers of his clothing
and with almost fastidious attention
washes each of the articles.
He spreads them flat on the granite rim to dry
and climbs naked into the water.

As he soaks
the grime of ages

melts from his hide.
He splashes his face
and scruffs his beard and hair.
Above the looming iron skeleton
a full moon shines upon the sleeping city.

The new day finds the man on the bus bench
his rebound bundles placed neatly beneath it.

The man is noticeably cleansed
his threadbare clothes less offensive.
He sits peacefully
listening to the street.
He raises his eyes to the sky
to see a lone bird soaring
above the city's reach.

There is distant music
lighthearted
nonsensical chanting
accented by the metallic jingle of a grocery cart.
The childish melody becomes clearer
a crosswalk away.

The clinking cart beats a staccato rhythm
as it enters the street.
Suddenly the rhapsody is broken.
A blaring dissonant horn
rips at the man's ears...
an endless screech of tires...
a cymbal crash...
and the music stops.

The demolished metal cart tumbles end over end,
spilling its insides into the street.
The cart skids to rest in the gutter near the bus bench
one of its wheels still spinning.

It thumps like a slowing heartbeat...
and dies.

The man sits
not moving.
Then he curls up on the bench
for a long sleep
beneath the brightly lettered advertisement:

Paradise Mortuary
Complete Caring Services - Low Cost Disposition
Removal Included.

ABOUT THE AUTHOR

I was born in Great Falls, Montana at the age of zero. One way or another, I expect to return to Big Sky when I get back to zero. I have spent a lifetime steeped in the Arts: first as an actor and a singer, then teaching Theatre Arts, and now painting and writing. Always, always there was poetry.

My fatherless childhood was not a smooth one by any measure. There was plenty of youthful angst, but also great joy and wonder. At the age of twelve, an amazing man came into my life and set me on a lifelong path...in the Arts. That man was my Drama teacher. He nurtured my talent, inspired and encouraged me. We are still in touch 60 years later.

As a teenager, I fell in love with girls and acting. The acting went well. I was also fortunate to have an impressive singing voice once it changed at around 15. When I reached my twenties, my acting talent opened many stage doors, including membership at the Arena Stage in Washington, D.C.

In time, I joined the National Touring Company of *Fiddler on the Roof,* followed by The Hedgerow Repertory Theatre in Philadelphia as resident set designer and leading man. I performed in numerous musicals including 300 performances as Don Quixote in *Man of La Mancha*. When I moved to Los Angeles in the 1970s I landed a lot of voiceover work dubbing films and television. A highlight was dubbing the voice of the villainous Bishop in Ingmar Bergman's five-hour epic, *Fanny and Alexander*.

A well-known hazard of pursuing an acting career is starvation. Believe me, I know. I have starved in some of the nation's finest cities. I can remember numerous times in New York City being down to pocket change and doing window displays on 5th Avenue to pay the rent on my one-room 6th floor walk-up. Eventually though, the years spent designing and building sets in repertory and regional theatres rescued me. By the time I reached Los Angeles, I had become an accomplished carpenter, and the building projects I did for many Hollywood notables helped to stave off hunger.

After many years in Theatre, I joined the Theatre Arts faculty at a prestigious Los Angeles private high school where for a quarter century, I designed and directed more than 75 productions as an Advanced Acting and Stagecraft teacher. What a wonderful gig it was, making Art with kids all day!

I now live in the East Mountains of New Mexico, where I have the time and freedom to pursue my other early passions – painting and writing poetry.

Reader be warned, I'm tossing in a commercial here. My paintings show in Santa Fe galleries as well as several galleries in Albuquerque. My portfolio can be viewed at my website at www.jeffwarrenartist.com.

This book is a compilation of some of my poems written across many years--of the highs and lows of my life. Like my paintings, they capture my thoughts about love and love lost, apostasy to whimsy. Some subjects are fanciful, others iconoclastic. You may even find an erotic one or three. Each poem expresses a moment, a thought or a dream in my life when I was so moved by love, tears, anger or laughter that I felt compelled to pen a poem. I hope I've done justice to those moments. Thank you for taking a moment to listen to what I've had to say.

Jeff Warren, 2015